Pro Resumes Made Easy

Andrea Drew

DEDICATION

Dedicated to job seekers around the world. Thank you for calling to tell me of your frustration – no funds for a pro resume writer due to unemployment yet desperately needing a professional resume. You are the inspiration for this book.
I know sometimes it can seem as though you are struggling to be seen or heard and next to impossible to land a job interview. Reading and applying the information in this book will see you well on the way to achieving that goal – I promise!

Dedicated also to my long suffering husband of 16 years, Steve. Whose wise words and calm advice give me the perspective I need to stay the course. Thank you for being you, and being the rock to your sometimes erratic "creative type" writer wife!

CONTENTS

Dedication

CHAPTER 1 SOME BASICS

What is the purpose of a resume? If you ask most people, they will tell you it is "to get a job interview." Yes, that's right it *is* designed to get you a job interview. But a resume is also designed to sell you, or generate enough interest in you to make the reader make contact and schedule a meeting time. Your resume has had enough impact, that out of the hundreds of resumes a recruiter receives in their email inbox daily, yours has stood out.

If you've heard the saying that recruiter's look at most resumes for between 5 and 20 seconds, it's true. Add to that equation the fact that resumes are now received via email inbox, and you need to consider the fact that this means that the top third of your first page will be the first thing the recruiter sees when they click open the attachment.

I'll be running you through the step by step process I use when writing a resume.

My resumes are written in a way that they;

a) Catch the recruiters eye immediately
b) Give them a reason to keep on reading
c) Stand out by writing them in a way that only 5% of all job applicants use effectively; and
d) Works with scanning software sometimes used by recruiters
e) Makes the reader want to meet with you!

CHAPTER 2 THE FIRST PART OF THE RESUME WRITING PROCESS - PLANNING

I'm sure most of you have lots and lots of questions including what headings to use, how long should it be, and do I include an objective and similar questions.

In my 11 years of writing resumes professionally, I've lost count of the number of questions that I have been asked about resumes.

Honestly, I think the best way to do this is for me to go through my resume writing process step by step, and then, when we're done, I'll include a list of possible questions and answers that may be still unanswered at the end of this book, OK? How does that sound? Good. OK, here we go.

The first thing to understand is that you don't need to include the word resume or curriculum vitae (CV) as a title within the document. What you are really telling the recruiter in doing so is that you really do think they are thick as two short planks, and that they are so dumb they don't even realise that this is your resume. No, don't go there. By the same token, you don't need headings or identifications such as name, address, telephone. It is obvious what they are! Surely people aren't that dumb? (Hold your tongue!)

Most resumes I see (and I have seen thousands) fall into the "shopping list" resume category. That is, they are a hastily written document scribbled down, and it is just a list of boring, general descriptions which mean little. The problem with this type of document is that it only describes the sort of duties that anyone in that position could do. There is nothing in there that markets you as a unique individual with value to bring to the potential employer.

Usually, when a client purchases a resume writing package online,

1

they also upload their current CV to me. At this point I acknowledge receipt of their payment and documents, and ask them to complete my in-house questionnaire.

Why do I do this?

Well most resumes are what I have rather cheekily termed "shopping list" resumes. That is, a quickly scribbled dry boring very general list of functions and responsibilities.

This does nothing to market the candidate, and actually really only talks about the types of functions anyone within that position could perform. A resume needs to talk about why you are different. What challenges or problems did you face, no matter how small? What did you do to solve these problems? And (hopefully) what was the fantastic result?

It is this information that I am really looking for when sending the questionnaire to a client. I also send them a video to guide them as to the "resume gold" that I am digging for.

Once I receive this, I get to work. I'm going to show you my process from start to finish, using the case study of "Angela" but firstly the planning stage. I usually write an action plan as this makes it easier to write the resume. It doesn't need to have all the boxes and look beautiful so long as you have the information there to work with.

Here is a sample:

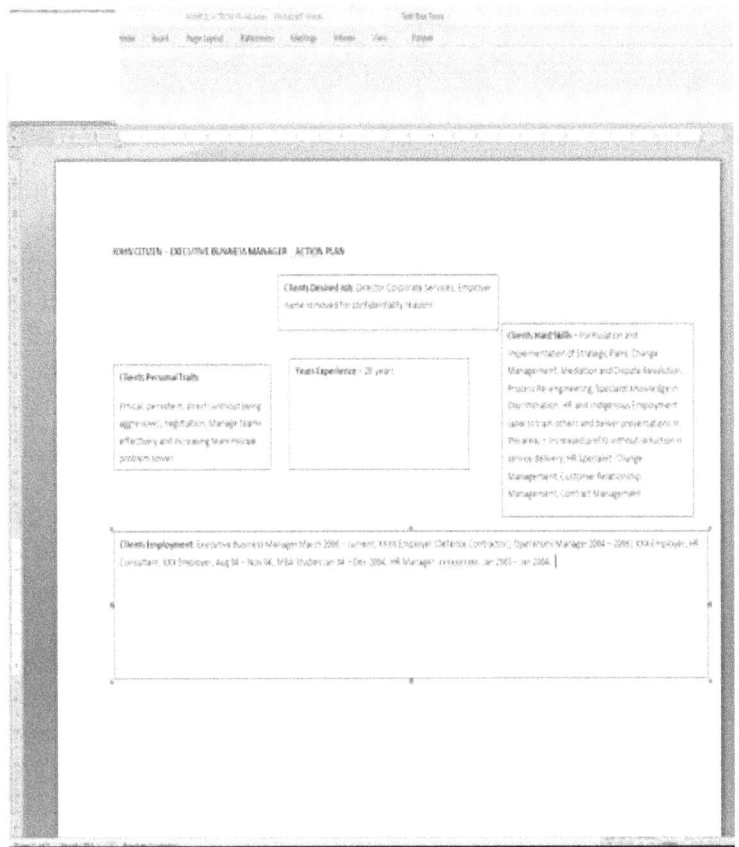

So you can see there I have the person's name – their position title, the position they are aiming for or targeting and their personal traits. Similarly I list the number of years' experience they have, as well as their "hard skills." These are their skills that I will be using to formulate a list of keywords within the resume, more on that to come. Hard skills list should only include those skills and ability that can be backed up by evidence. General skills are something most job seekers use a lot of; I see lots of words such as "team player" and "excellent organisational and prioritisation abilities" and most readers will scan over these if they look general without hard evidence.

What the job seeker doesn't realise is that almost every other job

3

seeker out there has done the same. Of course they don't realise this, as they don't get to see lots of CVs as I do (and lots of recruiters do) and so these statements lose impact. Statements such as "Contract Negotiation" and "Process re-engineering" or "Profit Maximisation" where this is backed up with evidence is much more powerful and makes the reader sit up and take notice, even if just for the fact that they very rarely see a resume of this kind.

Keywords are something that are not only used to attract the readers' attention, particularly in a situation where a recruiter is scanning through hundreds of resumes; they are also occasionally picked up by computer scanning software. Not all recruitment companies use this software, but those that do are able to search across their entire database of say 20,000 resumes through scanning for several keywords which may be for example, FMCG (fast moving consumer goods) or Contract Negotiations. So including "hard skills" here within the keywords section serves a dual purpose in that these words listed on the first page could more than likely assist you in gaining an interview, months after registering with a recruitment company. A position comes along, they interviewed you six months ago for a different position, and they registered your CV on their database and do a search and bang, up comes your resume in their search results months later!

Getting back to the action plan and resume writing, the second page of the action plan is where I plan the "meat" of the resume or achievements.

I use a tried and true method of CAR or Challenge, Action, Results. Here what I am doing is splitting up achievements into chunks to make sense of these prior to writing the resume. You will see here that these make up the bulk of the job seekers "story" and really demonstrate their skills:

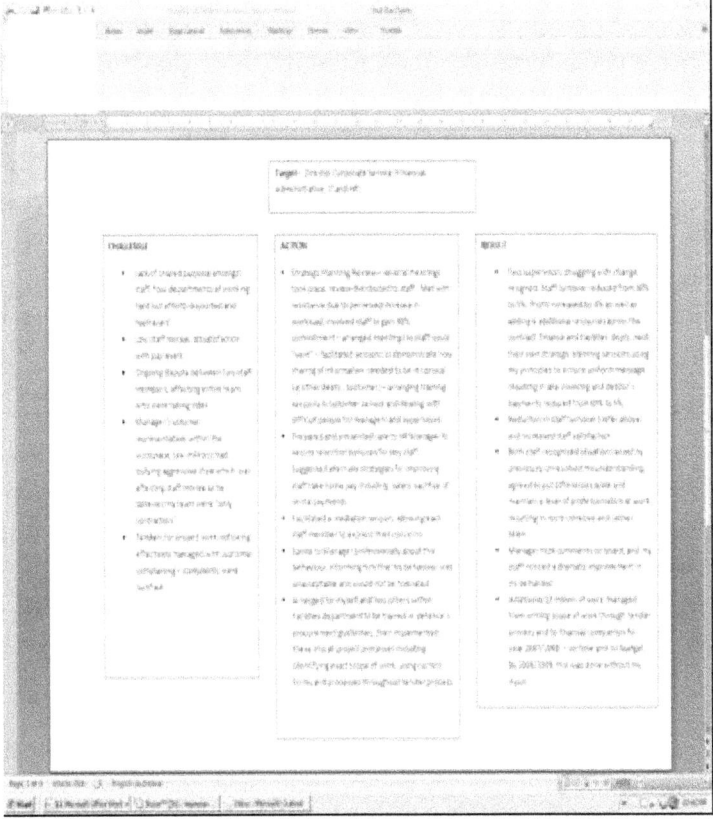

Here you can see the challenge, action result planning in action. As the above text is a little small, I thought I'd include a few of them here:

Challenge
- Lack of shared purpose amongst staff, four departments all working hard but efforts disjointed and haphazard

Action
- Strategic Planning Review – several meetings took place, review distributed to staff. Met with resistance due to perceived increase in workload, involved staff to gain 90% commitment – arranged meetings so staff could "vent" – facilitated sessions to demonstrate how sharing of information needed to be reciprocal (i.e. other depts., customer) – arranging training sessions in customer service and dealing with difficult people for managers and supervisors

Result
- Two supervisors struggling with change resigned, Staff turnover reduced from 30% to 5%, Profit increased by 3% as well as adding 4 additional resources across the contract, Finance and Facilities depts. Held their own strategic planning sessions using my principles to ensure uniform message, resulting in late invoicing and debtor's payments reduced from 60% to 5%

As you can see this is my rough "internal" text. From here it is a matter of tight phrasing, trying to get the salient points across to the reader without being too drawn out and long winded.

In this case the CAR approach became these two bullet points one after the other:
- Instigated and rolled out a series of strategic planning review meetings with outcomes distributed to staff. Allowed staff to communicate frustrations and concerns whilst simultaneously facilitating training sessions in customer service, and dealing with difficult people. Staff turnover reduced dramatically from 30% to 5% with a marked upsurge in morale and a more cohesive unit.

- Increased profit by 3% whilst adding five additional resources across the contract through formulation and rollout of strategic planning, staff training, facilitating staff meetings and demonstrating how improvements could be made

Here's another example of how a rough CAR planning point became a selling point within the resume:
Challenge:

- Tenders for project work not being effectively managed with customer complaining – complaints were justified

Action:

- Arranged for myself and two others within Facilities department to be trained in defence's procurement guidelines, then implemented these into all project processes including Identifying exact scope of work, using correct forms and processes throughout tender process

Result:

- Additional $3 million of work managed from writing scope of work through tender process and to financial completion for year 2007/2008 – on time and on budget. By 2008/2009 this was done without my input

Which when rewritten became the following:

- Recognised poor management of tenders for project work resulting in disgruntled client. Arranged two staff and myself to be trained in formal Defence procurement guidelines, implementing these into all project processes. Subsequently managed an additional $3 million in project work (estimated $7m in 2010/2011 financial year) throughout the entire tender process, enabling staff in following years to manage this process with minimal input

CHAPTER 3 WRITING THE RESUME

So now we have done our planning, we can get to writing. Remembering our earlier example, Angela is a graduate nurse, passionate about midwifery. She is trying to gain entry into this program. But her existing resume is just likes so many others I see, boring, ho hum, plain and in my opinion pretty useless (sorry Angela but I am sure you would agree with me □)

Right, well here is a snippet of the first section of the first page of her resume as it was:

CURRICULUM VITAE

Ashleigh Confidential
9 Example Street
xxxxxxxxxx
12345
0411 234 567
helpme@noidea.com.au

So what's wrong with that? You might be thinking. Well, here's what's wrong with it. Firstly, why does it need a heading or title of "Curriculum Vitae?" Shouldn't it be obvious to the reader what this is, after all they've already received an email in response to a job ad (most of the time) so the recruiter should know that you aren't sending them the latest cricket scores.

Unless, you really are desperately trying to tell the recruiter that you think they are stupid. No? I didn't think so.

The second thing is that this heading doesn't really stand out to me. Keep in mind that I was a recruiter in a previous life. Picture this. Your manager has put you in charge of the advertising and

9

screening process for 30 positions. Each position receives between 100 and 1000 applications including cover letters and resumes. So you really do only give each application about 5 to 30 seconds, meaning that the resume has to stand out immediately.

Combine this information with the fact that over the last thirteen years I have looked at thousands of resumes, and I can assure you that most resumes look exactly like the "before" resume listed here. Bland, boring, non-descript. When I write the resumes, I try to incorporate in the very top section of the document:

a)   Contact details of the candidate:

b)   A quick idea for the recruiter as to what sort of candidate they are dealing with e.g. Results focussed Accountant seeking auditors role (or similar)

c)   6-8 bullet points of "hard" skills

You can see below how I rewrote the very beginning of this clients resume:

ANGELA SIMPSON

Address removed for confidentiality reasons
Email: 123@123.com
Home: (01) 2345 6789 • Mobile: 0123 456 789

STUDENT/GRADUATE NURSE DRAWN TO MIDWIFERY

- Anticipated NSW Nursing Registration (List A) December 2009
- Women's health primarily pregnancy and birth
- Gynaecology and urology ward exposure

- Emergency Response tactician
- Received accolades for nursing essays
- Computer proficient (MS Office/Internet/Intermediate to Advanced)

A couple of things to remember:

1.   Only list "hard" skills. You may notice above I have listed these, which I discovered via Angela's questionnaire. Don't, don't please don't include wishy washy statements and "soft" skills such as "effective team skills" "outstanding communication" "ability to prioritise and manage time" I see these sorts of general meaningless statements all the time. Trust me, 99% of all resumes I see make these sorts of claims which, without evidence mean nothing! Every man and his dog will claim they have these skills.

2.   Don't go overboard with fancy graphics, fonts or layout. I say stick to black and white, with a regular font or typeface such as

Arial or similar. Yes, use bullets and bold or underline for emphasis, but don't go overboard. If you are using these for emphasis, they are no longer emphasised if the entire page is bold, or 75% or 50% of it is. Get the idea? Use bolding or underlining or italics sparingly and only where definitely needed. Also if you use bullets ensure these are uniform throughout the document and well formatted

3. Start bullet points or achievements using the CAR approach with a verb or strong action word e.g. revamped or collated or redesigned. Refer to the end of this eBook for a list of power words for use in your new resume.

From here you need to continue writing the resume, as outlined in the previous chapter, and using the CAR approach. Once your resume is completed, including an education and references section, have someone that you trust look over the resume to hopefully give an objective opinion. (Including me – refer to bonus section!)

Hint: Don't be tempted to use the same action word over and over in your resume. For example:

- Improved sales performance by 30% through implementing new sales force training program
- Improved customer relations through individualised follow up

To help you I've included a "power words" section at the end of this book to use when writing your bullet points/achievements.

CHAPTER 4 PROFESSIONAL HISTORY/EMPLOYMENT NARRATIVE

This is where you get into the "meat" of the resume and which is the recruiter's main focus. What is your experience, working background or as I sometimes call it "Career Snapshot"

Keep in mind here, that less is more. Truly. This is a marketing document designed to generate enough interest that the reader really wants to meet with you to find out more about you and what you are capable of.

That doesn't mean that you list out every single function of your job as well as outstanding achievements.

EMPLOYMENT HISTORY

June 04 – Oct 06   **Confidential Aged Care HOME: Some State**
Assistant Nurse

- To ensure the care needs of residents are identified and met, and that the environment of the home is conducive to excellent age care management.
- Working independently under the supervision of a registered nurse to carry out the personal care needs of the residents.
- Reporting on the needs of residents to the registered nurse, and providing information regarding changes in needs and abilities.
- Carrying out treatments / interventions, as per the residents nursing care plan.
- Ensuring the adherence of policies and procedures.
- To co-operate with the diversional therapist and recreational officers to facilitate the involvement of residents in social/ recreational activities.
- Escorting and ensuring the safety of mobility of the resident at all times.
- Participating in handover reports, recording and reporting relevant data. (Including incidents and accidents).
- Assisting with the ongoing review, formulation and implementation of improved work practices.

This is what Angela did within her resume. Let me ask you a question. Would you find reading through that text interesting? Does it grab your interest? No? Well then how can you expect a recruiter to see anything other than "boring" written all over it? How should this be written? Well personally I believe that accountabilities or functions can be discussed at interview if necessary. Duties and responsibilities are the sort of thing that *anyone* in that job could do.

What is going to sell or market you and your skills effectively? How do you demonstrate proof of your skills or evidence that you can do what you say you can? How can you position yourself as unique or the best person for the job? The CAR formula or;

- Challenge or problem
- Action – what did you do to solve it?
- Result – what was (hopefully) the result of your actions and overcoming the problem?

The trick here is to tell your "story" to the employer. In this way, not only do you provide evidence to the reader of your skills, but you set yourself apart from the pack. To demonstrate this a little better, I've included some statements where I managed to reword the job seekers information into something eye catching:

Before:

➢ Departments I manage are Emergency Services, Administration and Finance (includes IT), Facilities Management, and Commercial Operations

➢ My focus since moving from the Operations Manager to the Executive Business Manager's role has been to streamline processes and procedures with the aim of providing a more effective and consistent service to our contracted customer (Department of Defence) and to other stakeholders such as xxxxxx residents, xxxxxxx Test Facility Customers, and tourists and other visitors to the community. This has been achieved while still maintaining a healthy bottom line for the Company

Positive outcomes achieved to date include the development of a strategic plan for departments which has resulted in significant improvement in the timely processing of the finance functions; including a customer satisfaction survey process; development of an HR plan to improve our ability to retain and attract key staff , including a review of remuneration and benefits; development, in conjunction with the Facilities Management team, of a strategic plan for the management of contracted activities for the next 5 years; improved commercial opportunities for additional business; development and implementation of an improved, effective Helpdesk service, and the timely management of Project plans to meet key objectives of BAE Systems and the customer.

BORING!! Would you read through all of that if you had 99 other documents to read through?

And after:

xxxxxxxxxxx, State   03/2006–present

Executive Business Manager
Upon commencement, the challenges appeared daunting. Long standing customer difficulties combined with a four departmental team suffering lack of vision and failing to meet Key Performance Indicators prompted the need to develop a strategic plan and address customer shortfalls whilst improving profit, cash flow and staff morale and decreasing staff turnover.
Identified challenges including dissatisfied customers, backlogs in accounts payable and receivable, frequent staff turnover, and lack of shared vision.

- Instigated and rolled out a series of strategic planning review meetings with outcomes distributed to staff. Allowed staff to communicate frustrations and concerns whilst simultaneously facilitating training sessions in customer service, and dealing with difficult people. Staff turnover reduced dramatically from 30% to 5% with a marked upsurge in morale and a more cohesive unit.

- Increased profit by 3% whilst adding five additional resources across the contract through formulation and rollout of strategic planning, staff training, facilitating staff meetings and demonstrating how improvements could be made

Are you getting the idea? It's a matter of quantifying your achievements and giving *context* or "the story" based on the CAR approach. Employers are interested in results. Funnily enough, very few candidates manage to include these in their resume, less than 1% of all job seekers manage to do this. Simply including these results is enough to make you stand out from the pack. You may see above that I am telling the job seekers individual story. I state the problem or challenges, what was actually done to overcome these challenges, and the measurable, quantifiable result. Once you start talking about results or how you can add value, employers are all ears.
Another tip: always start each bullet point with a strong action word or verb. And don't use the same verb or action word over and over. Use the power words section at the end of this document liberally!

15

CHAPTER 5 WHERE TO FOCUS

I'm sure many of you are interested in where I put my focus within a resume? Well, it goes a little like this:

70% of the focus should be on the first page

20% of the focus on the second page

10% on the rest

Why?

The first page is what recruiters will look at primarily. They will make a snap, ten second decision on whether to continue reading. So this is the point of impact. They are also primarily interested in what the job seeker is doing now, and how they can add value. Give this information to them quickly and effectively with impressive wording and layout and you will have their interest.

I am going to include a sample here of a successful resume, so I can show you what I mean by where I place the focus.

Keep in mind that the samples I am showing you here have:

a)   Won the job seekers lots of interviews; and

b)   In many cases gained the job seeker their pick of job offers. One of these clients was offered more than one position from which to take their pick! Nice position to be in don't you think?

John Citizen
Details removed for confidentiality reasons
Email: sample@sample.com **Home**: (00) 9999 9999

X Director/ Satellite Analyst/X Engineer

Persistent trouble shooter, renowned for remaining calm under pressure. Specialist in crisis management, delivering simple solutions to complex problems. Excels at mentoring controllers and understanding complex needs and requirements. Employs a vast knowledge of design, development, integration and operations support of X/L-band payloads

- Collaborative team worker with mature and confident communication and liaison skills
- Energetic, enthusiastic and highly responsible leader
- Innovative problem solver

Career Highlights
Sample Employer – Melbourne, Victoria 1998 - 2010

This x communications company employs 200 staff worldwide, and 18 within the Melbourne office. This position reported to the Vice President Operations and supervised six staff. Initial employment in 1998 was as Quality Officer, whereupon I was promoted to Payload Engineer in 2000 and Mission Director in 2010

Mission Director (2004 – 2010)
Highlights include:
- Participated in conversion of all Payload procedures from an Astrium control system to an ISI (EPOCH) control system. This involved conversion, testing the completed procedure via a Dynamic satellite simulator and ultimately comparing bit patterns from the original procedure to the newly converted procedure using 'Wireshark.' During this process determined some procedures were not being converted correctly so wrote software to correct the conversion process using Visual Basic (VB)
- Analysed and identified failure on board Asiastar satellite resulting in switch off of an active unit and powering on of a redundant unit. After bringing the beam back online, edited all procedures that referenced the failed unit, and rewrote sections to

reference the new unit
- Improved payload recovery procedure from 8 hours to 2 hours by rewriting and streamlining procedures, removing redundant steps and speeding up various parts of the procedure
- Repositioned the North East beam resulting in better coverage over China
- Promoted to Mission Director from previous position as Payload Engineer

"Over the years, I always talked up the Melbourne mission, GCN and PFLS crew to the WS and FVI people here at HQ. You made things go really smoothly, even in the face of MCC trouble. I could always count on you for mastering any issues pertaining to channel activity on Asiastar. Also your creation and management of the PHP 'Satellite Anomaly DB' is really an excellent piece of software and has worked well from day one for us here in Washington."
Name Removed, Colleague,(Mission Director) Washington HQ, Sample Employer

Responsibilities included:
- Trained Payload engineer as well as 5 satellite Controllers
- Directed the satellite engineering team on payload reconfigurations and anomalies
- Managed daily operations of mission engineering and broadcast operations
- Maintained regular contact with ground stations in China Melbourne and Singapore as well as regular teleconferences with Washington head office

Sample Employer – Melbourne Vic
Payload Engineer (2000 – 2004)
Highlights included:
- Proposed and created a web site accessible by both Asian and African sites, in order to share satellite anomaly data, improving failure recovery time. Used MySQL, PhP and HTML to create the application, which is still in use today
- Wrote software application which automatically converted trend data into graphs using Visual Basic Application (VBA) and Visual Basic (VB). This saved large amounts of time as previous system meant manual retrieval of data and manual creation of graphs in Excel. As a result of this successful application was asked to extend its capability to graphing more complex plots
- Promoted to Payload Engineer from Quality Officer position

Responsibilities included:
- Supported Mission Director in monitoring and controlling channel programming, routine maintenance on feeder link station and day to day running of the mission segment

Sample Employer – Melbourne Vic
Quality Officer (1998 – 2000)
Highlights included:
- Resolved complaint of staff bullying and conflict. Initial complaint of racial abuse resulted in senior management proposing dismissal of two controllers. Negotiated with management to investigate the matter further, eventually determining that two staff members were targeting all controllers, rather than the behavior being personally or racially motivated. Counselling of two staff members ensured staff retention and dramatically improved morale.

Responsibilities included:
- Ensured on-site configuration changes and anomaly management were implemented in line with xxxxx quality requirements
- Performed operational impact assessment of procedures and indicated improvements where appropriate

pg. 19

- Implemented quality audits
- Executed operation qualification on Asia star satellite including procedures prior to launch
- Monitored all procedures and satellite tests, reporting anomalies, requesting changes and confirming all activities relating to operational qualification
- Coordinated with ground stations globally to line up carriers, and configure resources on board to broadcast their programs to one of three downlink areas in Asia
- Member of the Asia star launch and early orbit phase team (LEOP)
- Supervised controllers and coordinated all Controller related issues
- Facilitated smooth functioning of Regional Operations Centre during nominal operations

Sample Space Agency – Darmstadt, Germany 1995 - 1998
Analyst
Highlights included:
- Created web page in order to disseminate monthly performance reports to all European space agency sites, subsequent to Operations Manager request to disseminate monthly reports in an effective manner. This page is still in use at http://ersmonrp.esoc.esa.de/start.htm
- Acted as Ranging Officer for ESR1, and Quality Officer for ERS2 including monitoring data collection from a remote sensing station in Sweden, as well as ensuring the satellite was delivered to the owner in orbit, and functioning as expected
- Involved in all three satellite launches both in Europe and Australia. ERS1 and 2 (scientific satellites) and Asia star (communications satellite) including launch and early orbit phase.
Responsibilities included:
- Supported European Remote Sensing Satellite (ERS) ERS-1 and ERS-2 nominal and anomaly operations
- Managed both ground and space segment operations
- Assessed overall platform and payload health
- Trained new Controllers and assisted Spacecraft engineers with trouble shooting and report generation

Education

Bachelor of Information Technology (Networking)   Monash
University   completion 2010
(final semester)

Professional Development

Introduction to 3D Studio Max (Graphical Design software) RMIT
Melbourne   2002
Platform, Payload and Associated group equipment Alcatel,
Astrium and Xxxxx France 1998
User level Introduction to UNIX   ESOC
Darmstadt (Germany)   1997
Certificate in Spacecraft operations   ESOC
Darmstadt (Germany)   1994

Technology

Programming PhP, Java, JavaScript, HTML, VB, VBA, SQL
Operating Systems Windows, Linux, Unix Applications MS Office,
3D studio max, Flash, Dreamweaver

References

References removed for confidentiality reasons

This was only one sample, but I am hoping it is enough to give you an idea of what I am aiming for.

Do you notice how the bulk of the focus was on the first page, as well as the way the achievements were worded?

Recruiters really are interested in current positions first, keywords (in this case such as Satellite engineer, X/L band payloads). The focus when I write this resumes is firstly the current position, less so the one prior to that, and even less the one before that.

You may also notice that the word "I" isn't used in my resumes. That's because the resume is a marketing document. It should be written in the third person, and using the word "I" makes it first person.

From there I get into headings such as Education, Professional Memberships, Technology/IT skills (if applicable) Licenses and References. There are other possible headings, but we will get into those later in the book and in my "Q and A" section where I take up the most commonly asked questions over the last twelve years or so.

A couple of points I wanted to make about these last few sections though.

A) Only include education that is relevant to your career path or the position being applied for. Case in point. I once saw a resume received from a candidate seeking work within a large hospital as a Ward Clerk. She had in her education section information regarding her responsible service of alcohol certificate and her accreditation as TAB corp gambling processor. Hardly the sort of qualifications being sought by a hospital whose job it is to take care of patients often whom have been injured as a result of alcohol! Yes this may take you some time to amend for each resume, but it is worth it definitely, as to do otherwise is to give the recruiter the impression that you are adopting a "one size fits all" approach and are not checking your resume before sending it off to each application

B) Don't include professional memberships if you have not been a member for years. Stating that you were a member of the Law Society five years ago is not going to add value to your resume, as well as considering the fact that in all honesty memberships are not exactly a focal point of the resume (they are usually listed on the second or third page). Yes, definitely in the eyes of some recruiters memberships do carry weight, particularly when specified within their job advertisement or position description, but definitely not when the membership is lapsed.

I get asked whether it is better to list references individually or simply "Available on request." The answer is that this depends upon your individual situation, but most Australian employers according to survey, do prefer telephone referees listed within the resume. Refer also to the references chapter later on in the book.

CHAPTER 6 EDUCATION

This section can be set up much like the job experience section – it all really depends on what format you are choosing for your resume. This section is an important one for most students, and it is a required element of the resume. In this section, you should include:

▪ The name and location of your college or university

▪ Your degree and graduation date (although I don't recommend this for high school completion/Year 12 as some unscrupulous employers will use this to calculate your age which is illegal in most countries to discriminate based on these factors)

▪ Your major(s) and minor(s)

▪ Your marks and whether you attained a distinction, credit or similar

Use placement of information, bold type or underlining to highlight the features you want to emphasize but remember don't go overboard with it. It is sometimes necessary to pinpoint a feature or features that make you stand out among other students.

For example, students bold their university or college if they feel like that is a distinctive feature. Others may decide to bold their type of degree. When I am writing resumes for a graduate, I tend to mention this on the first page of the resume and discuss some of their outstanding projects to highlight their skills.

New graduates without a lot of work experience should list their educational information first. Alumni can list it after the work experience section.

Be sure the following is included in the education section of your resume:

▪ Your most recent educational information is listed first.

▪ Include your degree (A.S., B.S., B.A., etc.)

- Your major, institution attended, and your minor/concentration.
- Add your marks – e.g. credit or distinction if attained
- Mention academic honors.

Here are two examples of education sections, with different information emphasized.

Purdue University, West Lafayette, Indiana
Bachelor of Science May 1999
Major: Supervision; GPA 5.5/6.0 (Distinction)
Bachelor of Science in Accounting May 1999
Minor in Finance, GPA: 5.5/6.0 Major, 5.2/6.0 Overall (Distinction)
Purdue University, West Lafayette, Indiana

In your education section, you may want to include a couple of sub-groups – especially if you are a recent graduate looking for your first position. The first sub-group is "Related Course Work" or as I like to call it "Exemplary projects."

This is an optional part of your Education section, which can be quite impressive and informative for potential employers. Students seeking internships may want to list all completed major-related courses.

Graduates might list job-related courses different than those required to receive the degree (employers will already be aware of those). Include high-level courses in optional concentrations, foreign languages, and computer applications or communications classes. You may choose more meaningful headings such as "Technology Snapshot" if you wish to emphasise particular areas.

Remember employers and recruiters are familiar with the basic courses required in your major. Limit these sections to special courses or skills you have to offer.

Another optional sub-group in the education section is "Special Projects". This optional section may be added to point out special features of your education that are particularly interesting to employers or that may make you more qualified than others for the job you are seeking.

Students often include research, writing, or computer projects. Limit your description to the most important facts. You may expand your discussion in your application letter.

If you like, you can include any awards you received or special achievements in this section, but most resumes will have a separate section for this to cover not only academic awards but also business awards.

Our next section has to do with your special abilities as they apply to the position you are trying to gain.

CHAPTER 7 KEYWORDS AND ATTRIBUTES

While not all resumes contain a skills section, this may be helpful when you want to emphasise the skills you have acquired from your various jobs or activities, rather than the duties, or the job title but as stated earlier – only when backed up with results. However, a note: don't use keywords and attributes that are general and are not backed up with evidence based achievements. Attributes such as "effective team skills" or "good communication" are general and meaningless unless backed up with evidence. Use hard skills in this section.

If you do not have enough previous experience for a specific job you are seeking for, it is important to emphasise your skills pertaining to that job.

Skills can be just as important as work experience to employers. To prepare this section you should:

- List jobs, activities, projects and special offices.
- Think of skills you have gained through those experiences.
- Group these skills into 3 - 5 job related skills categories and use these as headings.
- List your skills with significant details under the headings.
- Arrange headings in order of importance as they relate to your goal.
- Arrange skills under headings in order of importance according to your goal.

In this section, you will also want to include any office machines you have experience operating, software programs you have become proficient in, and anything else that you feel might put in front for the application.

Example:

Leadership
- Conducted monthly club and board meetings for Lafayette Junior Woman's Club.
- Headed club's $8,000 philanthropic project sponsored by Tippecanoe County Historical Association.
- Coordinated responsibilities of committees to sell and serve food to 1500 people at fund raiser.

Business Communication
- Completed a formal report for Business Writing course.
- Wrote annual state and district reports of all club's community service projects, volunteered hours and monetary donations.
- Compiled type mimeographed and distributed club books to each member.

Financial Management
- Supervised the collection and dispersion of $4,000 in funds to various agencies and projects.
- Wrote and analysed periodic business statements regarding funds to specific projects/agencies.

The next section can be worded in a couple of different ways. Here is where you want to let the potential employer know you have participated in activities and events as well as that you are a member of professional organizations along with any special awards that you have received.

A lot of this depends on whether or not you are fresh out of school looking for your first job or if you have been in the business world and are applying for another job.

Note: A point to remember, including dates for education can in some cases provide information in relation to your age to unscrupulous, discriminatory employers, particularly if many years ago. Some will calculate your age based on the date you list for finishing school, so use judgment when including education dates

CHAPTER 8 VOLUNTEER WORK

You can choose a few different ways to word this section. If you like, it can be titled "Community Contributions" or "Awards and Organisations". It really is up to you. You have to tailor your resume to your specific needs as well as towards what type of job you are applying for.

This optional section points out your leadership, sociability and energy level as shown by your involvement in different activities. This should be your shortest section and should support your career goals and the positions you are targeting. Additional information about activities can be included in your application letter or discussed at your interview.

You should:
- Select only activities and honours that support your career objective.
- List your college or professional organisations and arrange them in order of importance as they relate to your career objective.
- Include any office or official position you held.
- Spell out any acronyms your employer may not recognise.
- Include dates.

Example:
Accounting Club, President
Alpha Zeta Professional Fraternity
Purdue Grand Prix Foundation, President
Purdue Association for the Education of Young Children (PAEYC)
For any activities, you should include the year you were involved. You also may want to include a brief explanation of the criteria

that you had to meet in order to get that honor.

Finally, you will wrap up your resume with a references section.

CHAPTER 9 REFERENCES

You will want to have several different people on hand who will vouch for you as far as your character, your work habits, your work ethics, and your general value and worth as an employee and person.
You will want to have a minimum of two references and no more than five.

The first rule of thumb for references is to ask the person first if you can use them as a reference when applying for jobs. As long as you have a good relationship with them, most people are happy to oblige for you and give you a glowing recommendation.

The purpose of a reference section is to have a list of people who can verify and elaborate on your professional experience for a potential employer. Past employers, professors, and advisors are the best professional references to have.

It is important to have a reference sheet because potential employers will often ask for a list of references they can contact. If you included a statement such as "References Available upon Request" on your resume, you should be able to produce a reference sheet as soon as one is requested. In any case, having a reference sheet will save you time later on during the interview process.

Make sure to include people who know what type of person you are and who are familiar with your work. It is important to select individuals who know your distinctiveness so that they can provide a positive and accurate description of you to the employer or company in which you are seeking employment.

You should ALWAYS contact your references before including them on a reference sheet. It is also a good idea to give them a copy of your resume and talk to them about the job you are seeking so they will know how to best represent you.

When you are listing your references, you should include the following information:

- Your name
- Your present and permanent address(es)
- Your reference person or persons' information, which includes that person's:
  - Name
  - Department/Company
  - Title/Position
  - Address
  - Telephone number
  - Brief statement as to how you know this person.

It is not required that you include the last part – the statement as to how you know this person, but it can help particularly if the relationship is not obvious. That way if a potential employer does check your references, they know why you wanted to list them on your reference sheet.

Another very important part of the job application process is the cover letter that you will include with your resume.

CHAPTER 10 THE COVER LETTER

The purpose of a cover letter is to introduce you and your resume as well as give some additional information about yourself to potential employers. You may also want to point out some parts of your resume you want the employer to pay special attention to.

An individually written cover letter typically accompanies each resume you send out. Your cover letter may make the difference between obtaining a job interview and having your resume ignored. It makes sense to devote the necessary time and effort to write effective cover letters.

A cover letter should complement, not duplicate your resume. Its purpose is to interpret the data-oriented, factual resume and add a personal touch. A cover letter is often your earliest written contact with a potential employer, creating a critical first impression.

There are three different kinds of cover letters:

- The application letter responds to a specific job opening you have seen advertised
- The prospecting letter inquires about any job openings
- The networking letter which requests information and assistance in your job search

If you are sending out a resume, your application cover letter should always include a line in your cover letter that says where you found the advertisement for the job you are applying for. If you saw it in a newspaper, be sure to underline the name of the newspaper (grammar rules count!)

You should always tailor your cover letter to the specific job you are applying for. It's certainly easier to write generic or blanket cover letters than it is to write a cover letter specifically targeted to each position you apply for. However, if you don't invest the time in writing cover letters you're probably not going to get the interview, regardless of your qualifications.

My first tip in writing a cover letter that works is to make a match between your qualifications and education with the job. This takes some time and effort and it's not always easy, but, it's important. Take the job posting and list the criteria the employer is looking for.

Then list the skills and experience you have. Either address to how your skills match the job in paragraph form or list the criteria and your qualifications.

Do not design a form letter and send it to every potential employer (you know what you do with junk mail!).
Effective cover letters explain the reasons for your interest in the specific organisation and identify your most relevant skills or experiences (remember, relevance is determined by the employer's self-interest). They should express a high level of interest and knowledge about the position.

To be effective, your cover letter should follow the basic format of a typical business letter and should address three general issues:

1.   First Paragraph - Why you are writing
2.   Middle Paragraphs - What you have to offer
3.   Concluding Paragraph - How you will follow-up

In some cases, you may have been referred to a potential employer by a friend or acquaintance. Be sure to mention this mutual contact, by name, up front since it is likely to encourage your reader to keep reading!

If you are writing in response to a job posting, indicate where you learned of the position and the title of the position. More importantly, express your enthusiasm and the likely match between your credentials and the position's qualifications.

If you are writing a prospecting letter a letter in which you inquire about possible job openings - state your specific goal. Since this type of letter is unsolicited, it is even more important to capture the reader's attention.

If you are writing a networking letter to approach an individual for information, make your request clear. The advantage to writing a letter like this and including your resume is that you will be making contacts in the business world and when a job opening comes up, they may still have your resume on file. It never hurts to be pro-active when looking for a job!

In responding to an advertisement, refer specifically to the qualifications and requirements listed and illustrate how your particular abilities and experiences relate to the position for which you are applying. In a prospecting letter express your potential to fulfill the employer's needs rather than focus on what the employer can offer you.

You can do this by giving evidence that you have researched the organisation thoroughly and that you possess skills used within that organisation.

Emphasize your achievements and problem-solving skills. Show how your education and work skills are transferable, and thus relevant, to the position for which you are applying.

Close by reiterating your interest in the job and letting the employer know how they can reach you and include your phone number and/or email address. If you want, you can make a bid directly for the job interview or informational interview and indicate that you will follow-up with a telephone call to set up an appointment at a mutually convenient time. Be sure to make the call within the time frame indicated.

In some instances, an employer may explicitly prohibit phone calls or you may be responding to a "blind want-ad" which precludes you from this follow-up. Unless this is the case, make your best effort to reach the organisation. At the very least, you should confirm that your materials were received and that your application is complete.

If you are applying from outside the employer's geographic area you may want to indicate if you'll be in town during a certain time frame (this makes it easier for the employer to agree to meet with you).

In conclusion, you may indicate that your references are available on request. Also, if you have a portfolio or writing samples to support your qualifications, state their availability.

So, we've covered the three most important documents you need in a job search: the resume, the cover letter, and the reference sheet. Before you get excited and start mailing out your creations, there are some things that you need to do prior to that.

CHAPTER 11 MAKING SURE YOU ARE READY

You are trying to get a job and you are all-ready with your resume, reference sheet, and cover letter. Before you get all excited and put your info in the mail, you will want to go through a few check points.

First and foremost, run a spell check on your computer. But don't stop there. Read your documents over and over to make sure there are no typographical or grammatical errors. It might also help to have someone else read over them as well to be sure that it looks the way it should.

The more people who see your resume, the more likely that misspelled words and awkward phrases will be seen (and corrected).

Here is a checklist to keep in mind for your cover letter:

- The contact name and company name are correct
- The letter is addressed to an individual, if possible
- The cover letter mentions the position you are applying for and where it was listed
- Your personal information is all included and correct
- If you have a contact at the company, mention him or her in the first paragraph of your cover letter
- The cover letter is targeted to the position you are applying for
- The letter is focused, concise, clear, and well organised
- If you have a gap in your employment history, explain it in your cover letter
- The font is easy to read
- No spelling or grammatical errors
- Read the cover letter out loud to make sure there are no missing words
- You have kept a copy for yourself

When it comes to your resume, there are also a few things to keep in mind. Much is the same as for the cover letter, but you want your resume to be tip top as well. Here's a check list:

- There are no typographical or spelling errors
- The format is consistent throughout the entire document
- If printing, use a good quality, heavier paper – heavier than regular copy paper
- Print on only one side
- Use a font between 10 and 14 – you want it to be easy to read and look pleasant to the eye
- Use non-decorative fonts, but don't be afraid to experiment and use something a little interesting – just not TOO interesting!
- Stick to one font
- Avoid italics, scripts, and underlined words except for when underlining your headings
- Do not use horizontal or vertical lines, graphics, or shading.
- Do not fold or staple your resume.
- If you must mail your resume, put it in a large envelope and mail flat
- Be sure there is enough postage on the envelope to make it to the company
- When at all possible, deliver your resume in person and ask to speak with the personnel director when you do so.
- Follow up after a reasonable period of time if you have not heard anything. This shows initiative on your behalf and makes you memorable in the mind of the person doing the hiring.

Well, we've done a lot of talking about how to craft a resume and cover letter that gets attention. You probably want to see some more samples of what I am talking about, don't you?

CHAPTER 12 MORE RESUME SAMPLES

There are literally hundreds of different ways you can write a resume and so many formats you can use, it can be mind boggling. There are a lot of places on the Internet that can provide you with free templates that just require you to insert your personal information and then print it out. But feel free to use a few of these sample resumes that I like! True – they are not the known winning ones I have included that I wrote personally – but they are some of the better ones that I don't mind as far as samples and templates go.

If you are applying for a creative job, it is all right to be creative with your resume, but not too creative. A professional position, however, necessitates a professional resume.

Whichever way you decide to go, be sure to have your resume be eye catching and intriguing. As we have said, the resume is your first introduction to your potential employer, so you will want to make the best first impression that you can right out of the gate.

Do some research and look for various formats that you can try with your own resume. There are many, many places on the Internet that offer up free templates where you can just fill in your own information and you are on your way.

I was able to find all sorts of places that offered up resume samples to use as guidelines to follow when you are typing up your own resume. Although I don't generally recommend using samples, these are some of the better ones I found.

So, I offer up to you a few samples for you to consider when crafting a resume. Take them and use them as if they were your own.

RANDI B. JENKIN

134 Whaler Cove • Port Washington, NY 12345 • 123-555-1234 • rbjenkins@.bamboo.co

OBJECTIVE: Marketing or Marketing Management Position

HIGHLIGHTS OF QUALIFICATIONS

- May 2004 received M.B.A. Degree with emphasis in Marketing.
- Six years' experience in program development, international marketing, and Internet marketing.
- Highly effective leading and motivating teams to produce positive results while meeting deadlines.
- Strong communication, interpersonal, and presentation skills.

PROFESSIONAL MARKETING EXPERIENCE

COMTROTRON, New York, NY   2003 to 200-
Marketing Consultant / Graduate Student Intern
- Interned as marketing consultant for this international e-business development company.
- Became integral team member in the development of online marketing programs for clients including AT&T, Avon, and Nike.
- Developed reports for clients including Avon's "Customer Needs and Reports Strategy."
- Conducted extensive research on the Internet, analyzed information, identified online solutions, and reported results to project leaders and clients.

COOKING TIME INTERNATIONAL PUBLICATIONS, New York, NY   1998 to 200?
Publicity Manager
- Managed promotions and publicity campaigns for over 200 titles of international publishing company.
- Created promotional strategy, managed company website, and increased online promotions.
- Organized and conducted trade show presentations, promotional events, and seminars.
- On several occasions made guest appearances as a food expert for local network TV and radio stations.
- Made presentations on new directions and products at national and international cooking conferences.
- Supervised and trained staff of four including a publicist and marketing assistant.
- Pitched stories and secured placement in top 100 daily newspapers and high-profile magazines.
- Coordinated distribution of collateral such as catalogs, brochures, and point-of-sale materials.

LONDONMIST FRAGRANCES, London, England   1997 to 199?
Assistant to Publicity Director / Student Intern
- Assisted in coordination of promotional campaign that launched EveningMist line product, "Shades."
- Maintained departmental records and correspondence, coordinated and scheduled meetings.

EDUCATION AND TECHNICAL SKILLS

M.B.A., Marketing, New York University, New York, NY   200-

Relevant Coursework	Brand Management	Marketing Strategy	Sales Channel Mgt
Data Analysis	Sports & Events Mktg	Global Management	Strategic Advantage
Leadership	Decision Modeling	Managerial Finance	Managerial Accounting

B.A., History, Adelphi College, Garden City, NY   199?

Technical Skills - Illustrator, Photoshop, Filmaker, MS Access, Excel, PowerPoint, QuarkXpress

CHLOE ZABATSKI

123 Alpha Street • Las Vegas, NV 12345 • (123) 555-1234 • chloez@bamboo.com

OBJECTIVE: Position as Personal Assistant / Office Manager

HIGHLIGHTS OF QUALIFICATIONS

- 15+ years experience providing outstanding administrative and personal support to a senior executive.
- A motivated self-starter, able to quickly grasp issues and attend to details while maintaining a view of the big picture. Expert in juggling multiple projects and achieving on-time completion within budget.
- Creative, resourceful and flexible, able to adapt to changing priorities and maintain a positive attitude and strong work ethic.
- A clear and logical communicator, able to establish rapport with both clients and colleagues, and motivate individuals to achieve organizational objectives.

PROFESSIONAL EXPERIENCE

1988-pres.   **PERSONAL ASSISTANT & OFFICE MANAGER**
Paige & Associates, Denver, CO

Personal Assistant

- Provided continuous, high quality support to President/CEO. Coordinated schedule, appointments and travel arrangements; managed expense account and recovery.
- Proofed and edited speeches, reports and press releases; screened calls and communicated directives to Board members and company shareholders.
- Managed President's securities portfolio and prepared regulatory filings as needed. Acted as liaison to stockbrokers, accountants and legal counsel.
- Organized annual shareholder meetings, including site selection, catering and preparation of appropriate materials.
- Planned two major relocations: Assisted in site selection, worked with architect on interior design, and oversaw equipment/furniture/telecommunications setup without interruption in operations.

Office Manager

- Coordinated work flow among five consultants and supervised three support staff. Prioritized and delegated tasks, provided motivation and direction to create a positive work environment and ensured accurate, on-time completion.
- Tracked office expenses and created monthly reports for senior executive. Prepared invoices, Accounts Receivable/Payable and banking.
- Mediated conflicts among employees and between staff and management, utilizing diplomacy and humor to resolve issues.
- Responded to client needs and provided additional support where necessary.

Additional experience includes:
Seminar and Retreat Coordinator, Meditation, Inc., Reno, NV
On-site Massage Therapist, Reno Corporate Massage, Reno, NV

EDUCATION & TRAINING

B.A., Psychology, American University, Washington, DC
CMT / Somatic Educator, Somatic Institute, New York, NY
Additional training includes: Stress Management and Meditation

CHAPTER 13 - SAMPLE COVER LETTERS

As I've said, the cover letter can be just as important as the resume, so you will want it to look as professional and intriguing as it can. I have a sample letter here that you may want to use to refer to when crafting your own cover letters.

Mr Test Example
Street Address
Suburb State and postcode
Tele: (00) 0000 0000
Mobile: 0000 000 000

16 August 2013

Sample receiver details

Dear Mr Test

RE: ACCOUNT MANAGER / BUSINESS DEVELOPMENT MANAGER / PROCUREMENT FOR GLOBAL FMCG – REFERENCE: VN-717900

• The educational background, experience, and skills listed in your recent advertisement on www.seek.com.au are only the beginning of what I can bring to this role.

• I have sound account management and business development skills, an acute eye for detail and an ability to recognise opportunities for growth and diversification. I enjoy liaising and negotiating with clients and possess strong client relationship consolidation skills and an understanding of their needs. I am adaptable and versatile and am able to comprehend deadlines and strive to meet them. As part of my role with Phillips Foods Inc., my key responsibilities included the development and implementation of strategic business plans, the identification of new opportunities to support ongoing growth and I built and managed internal/external partnerships to ensure effective delivery of objectives. I was also responsible for building and maintaining a positive team environment, and implemented risk strategies and received positive business outcomes.

• I have over ten years experience in business development, marketing and business management which effectively enables me to perform and deliver exceptional outcomes.

• My resume is enclosed as proof that I meet all the criteria listed in your advertisement and an interview would give me the chance to further demonstrate my unique strengths. I am available for an interview at a time of your convenience.

Sincerely,

Mr Example

CHAPTER 14 - SAMPLE REFERENCE SHEETS

Note: References sheets are used more in the USA than in Australia where references are included within the resume itself at the end of the document.

Your reference sheet is important to have as well – like I stated earlier. While this will not be forwarded along with your resume and cover letter, you will still need to have it on hand during an interview so that you can produce it when your potential employer asks for it.

Here are some sample reference sheets for you when creating your own reference sheet.

CARRIE E. COMPLETE
PRESENT ADDRESS
123 Hawkins Graduate House
West Lafayette, IN 47906
(317) 555-1123
Indianapolis, IN 46220
(317) 555-1829

REFERENCES
Professor John English
Sociology Department
Purdue University
Stone Hall
West Lafayette, IN 47907
(317) 555-6000
Professor English is my academic advisor and is presently supervising my research in an independent study sociology course.

Mrs. Diana Handie
Food Services Supervisor
Hawkins Graduate House
Purdue University
West Lafayette, IN 47907

(317) 555-2323
Mrs. Handie was my supervisor when I worked in the Hawkins Cafeteria.

Mrs. Jennifer Active
Activity Therapy Staff Wabash Valley Mental Health Center
2900 North River Road
West Lafayette, IN 47906
(317) 564-9600
Mrs. Active is my current employer.

References for James Esterman
433 Colby Hall
Hutchinson University
Hutchinson, IL 60353
(847-555-2733)
esterj01@hutch.edu

Dr. Pat Wombat
Professor of Psychology
Hutchinson University
Hutchinson, IL 60353
wombatp@hutch.edu
(847-555-3212)

Dr. Wombat was my supervisor in
the Human Subjects Research Lab.

Dr. Chris Murphy
Professor of Biology
Hutchinson University
Hutchinson, IL 60353
(847-555-2733)
Dr. Murphy was my professor in
Biology 425: Special Research Projects.

Mr. Michael McCollins
Project Director

The Acme Corporation
112221 Main Street
Hutchinson, IL 60353
(847-555-2813)
Mr. Murphy supervised my internship
at the Acme Corporation.

Ms. Sonia Ramirez
Manager
The Rasmussen Corporation
1192 Elston Avenue
Chicago, IL 60105
(312-555-2733)
SRamirez@rasmussen.com
Ms. Ramirez supervised my co-op
experience at the Rasmussen Corporation.

IM A SAMPLE
1234 North 55 Street
Bellevue, Nebraska 68005
(402) 292-2345
iasample@aol.com

PROFESSIONAL REFERENCES
Name
Position
Title
Company
Address City, State, Zip Code
Company Phone Number

So you have your resume out there and you got the phone call for an interview. This next section will be brief, but there are some things to keep in mind when you are face to face with a prospective employer during a job interview. Hopefully, my advice will help you get the job!

CHAPTER 15 - THE INTERVIEW

The first thing that you want to remember when you are at a job interview is that first impressions count. Dress appropriately for the job. No matter what, though, never wear jeans to a job interview – it doesn't matter how casual the job is that you are applying for, jeans are inappropriate in any situation.

For women, a nice skirt and dress or a suit is what you should wear. For men, a suit is most appropriate, but you can get away with a pair of khaki pants and a nice polo shirt.

When you are talking to your interviewer, be enthusiastic about the job. Convey your excitement about the possibility of working for this company and always, always smile.

If you are applying for a creative position or a teaching position, you might want to bring along a portfolio of your work so that you can show off your creativity. Having samples of what you can do can make you stand out over other applicants.

Above everything else, be excited and enthusiastic about your possible job. When you are happy about being there, it will show in your demeanor and your responses. I can't stress enough how much this can make a difference in getting the job and not getting the job.

Your job interview is when you get the chance to shine. Be sure and answer all of the questions accurately and with enthusiasm. Try not to hesitate and be prepared for anything. This writer once had an interview for a sales position where the interviewer asked me to sell him a pen. I was able to think on my feet and gave him a great sales pitch. I got the job!

You can be just as successful as I was when you take the time to be prepared for your interview and then shine during the talk you are having with the person doing the hiring. It is truly your personality that will get you the job along with your experience and your education.

Once you get the interview, it is all up to you, but you can do it. The person interviewing you already knows a lot about you from your perfectly crafted resume that we have taught you how to put together.

CHAPTER 16 - FREQUENTLY ASKED QUESTIONS AND RESUME NO NO'S

1. How long should a resume be?

The answer to this truthfully is as long as it needs to be. Having said that you also don't need something 6-10 pages long, that tells me that there is lots of unnecessary information in there that isn't adding value to the document. Use the above principles and you should get something around 3-4 pages for most job seekers, 1-2 pages for a graduate. The only exception to this is in the UK where they are fixed on the magic number of 1-2 pages for all CVs (they don't call them resumes over there; they think that is an absolutely hilarious term!)

2. Should I include a resume objective?

A contentious issue and one I discuss at great length in an article on my website. Personally I don't use them nor do I include them, reason being I believe that resumes are there to sell your skills, attributes and a sense of how you can add value to the company. I know personally, when recruiting, I am more interested in what they can bring that what they're objectives are. Yes it is somewhat of interest, but it is not a major factor.

3. Should I include clip art or graphics within the resume?

Definitely not! (Unless you are a graphic designer in which case I recommend a separate portfolio) The furthest I would go in this regard would be to include a bar graph where a job seeker has achieved stellar results, but that would be as far as it goes, anything else has a tendency to look tacky.

4. What about pictures? I've been told by a friend that it is good to include a picture of myself to help me stand out

Ah yes, that old chestnut, my friend told me. At this point I rudely think (but don't say) it sounds like your friend is an instant expert, just add water. Oops, there I've said it. Oh well! I don't recommend including pictures of yourself primarily because this is subliminally saying that you consider your appearance to play a large part in whether you are being selected or not. The exceptions to this are professions of course such as modelling or flight attendant where these factors of course will be important. But in my humble opinion, it is best not to go there at all.

5.   I'm studying currently, how do I include this within my resume?

That's simple, state for example, Master of Business studies, Melbourne University, anticipated completion July 2014 or something similar

6.   Can I include character references rather than professional?

Hmm, how can I put this without seeing a little abrupt? A potential employer, when they ask a referee what your management style is, do not necessarily want to hear what a great friend you are and how you are always there at the football matches manning up the canteen, reliable as clockwork. Character references are not that useful, it is automatically assumed that you are of good character when you are offered the position. You need a couple of referees willing to talk about your performance when called – at the very worst this should be a colleague who has knowledge of your working performance and style.

COMMON RESUME BLUNDERS

Here is a list of common errors and notes I made during a recent resume critique – be sure to avoid these in your name!
•   Problem with name. Name Text is hot pink, garish and difficult to read. It should be no larger than 14 point and in Arial or Times New Roman black or similar with name in bold text.
•   Problem with contact details each one has the title before it for example address: then address Town" xxx . I would remove the title for each set of contact information
•   Problem with font colour and uniformity. In contact section, the font is pink and is not in line or uniform with the rest of the

document. I would change it to black times roman and bold the name.

- Problem with alignment of mobile phone details. These are not in correct alignment and look odd when compared to email details below. I would set these cell phone details as a right aligned tab

- Problem with lack of indication of type of profession within the resume for example "Senior Marketing Executive" which is usually placed towards the very top of the resume. In this case I would insert text centred and bold just under contact details stating "Senior Marketing Officer/Business Development Strategist" or similar

- Problem with Objective. This is very general and non-specific and isn't adding to the resume at all; also it has a heading of Objective: xxx which is not needed. I would delete the entire objective

- Problem with Summary. The heading prior to text start of "Summary: xxx" is not needed and unnecessary. I would delete the heading

- Problem with summary text, (under objective) sentences seem very long and unwieldy. I would reword the summary into a shorter and sharper section.

- Problem with last two sentences of summary text. These sentences are general and non-specific and not adding anything to the resume, I would delete these two sentences "Possess excellent communication and interpersonal skills." And "A team player, reliable, organized and punctual"

- Problem with Professional Inventory section. Bullets vary between past and present tense for example "Devised Special Promotions" and "Developing Databases" and "Supervised Teams" I would delete these as all bullets need to be in same tense

- Problem with Professional Inventory Section, Business Development is included twice; I would remove one of these bullets.

- Problem with Professional Inventory Section bullet entitled Excellent Communication Skills is very general and non-specific. I would delete this bullet

- Problem with Professional Inventory section a number of

bullets are not in the same tense as other bullets and/or do not communicate "hard skills" and so need to be deleted. I would delete the following "Developing Databases, Supervised Teams" and "Product Pricing Structures"

- Professional Inventory section Three Bullet points sound very similar "strategic marketing, market planning and coordinating marketing plans" would merge these into one bullet point "Strategic Market Planning"

- Problem in Experience Highlights section. Bullets are not uniform and are different to those used within the Professional Inventory section. Would change these bullets to black squares as used in previous section to maintain uniformity of bullet type

- Problem in Experience highlights section. Bullet entitled Event Management is not aligned with other bullets, I would realign this so that all bullets match up vertically

- Problem with Event Management bullet in Experience Highlights Section. Words used are "responsible for a trade mission to China" – responsible for is bland and is something that should never be seen in a resume. I would delete this first sentence and reword bullet to "Led trade mission to China, arranging meetings and educating local teams to overcome cultural barriers" would also ask client for result of this trade mission to incorporate into this bullet

- Error in Career Summary section – date for Logan City Council is not in vertical alignment with dates below it. Would realign this date

- Problem with Career Summary Section – McDonalds Restaurants – the dates for this employment span 22 years, and are not only unrelated to a business marketer, but they give a negative age assumption about the candidate. I would delete this employment altogether

- Problem in Employment Narrative Range view City Council section – salary is mentioned (salary $54K plus benefits) this should not be included within a resume and should be deleted. Salary is something that would be negotiated between applicant and employer at a later stage not included in the resume

- Problem in summary of range view city council (employment narrative) end of 2nd paragraph text includes reason for leaving –

accepted redundancy….this should be deleted and not included within the resume as it could create negative assumptions with the reader (e.g. we can employ them at a lesser salary for example) and should not be included in the resume

- Problem within Range View City Council in Employment Narrative section – employment dates are poorly aligned and look like different font sizes, these should all be right aligned and the same font
- Problem within Range View City Council in Employment Narrative section – first sentence under position titles starts with "responsible for" which should be deleted and replaced with "Steer marketing initiatives from ….". Number of bullets do not start with a verb or action word
- Problem with 3rd bullet point down in Range view City Council employment, employment narrative. Bullet commences with text "duties include" which is not helping within the resume I would delete the text "duties included" and change educating to "educated" as the first word of this bullet point
- Problem with last bullet point Range view City Council in employment narrative section. This bullet commences with "Develop a network" and seems to be in present tense rather than paste tense as all other bullets are. Would change word develop to developed
- Problem with Global Languages Incorporated employment in Employment Narrative section. Dates and positions titles are confusing the way they are formatted, difficult to determine which dates belong with which text. I would a) move date 2/200-2/2005 to far right via right aligned tab. Right align date for project manager position (4/2001-2/2005), place Graduate Marketer position title on next line hard left with dates right aligned. Delete salary 35K as this information could work against the candidate and should not be included
- Problem in Global Languages Inc in employment narrative section, first line begins "Responsible for" delete this text and rewrite sentence to beginning "Developed marketing plan…."
- Problem in Global Languages Inc in employment narrative section, 2nd paragraph includes line "Reason for Leaving…" this sentence should be deleted as this information could go against the

candidate

- Problem in Global Languages Inc in employment narrative section last bullet point is in present tense e.g. "Eliminate translation errors and reduce…" this should be reworded to past tense e.g. "Eliminated translation errors and reduced"
- Problem in Education|Training section, second line includes irrelevant training which will work against the candidate e.g. "Training includes Macramé course….Baby "Green" this entire line/sentence should be deleted
- Problem with Personal section. None of this information is relevant to the candidate's ability to take on a new role and would actively work against the candidate. The entire section including date of birth, marital status and hobbies in their entirety should be deleted.
- Employer names are different between the employment summary and the actual descriptions achievements which will be alarming to the reader e.g. "What do dates match but not employer names? What is the candidate trying to hide?"

If you have other questions that haven't been answered so far, feel free to email me andrea@career-chick.com.au – I'd be happy to hear from you.

And before we move on to the next section, another sample – just for good measure, in fact you might recognise these as being the finished product based on the sample action plan I referred to earlier!………

Andrea Drew

JANE CITIZEN

Sample address   01 2345 6789
Nowhereville sample@sample.com

EXECUTIVE BUSINESS MANAGER

Strategic Planning | Change Management | Process Re-engineering

"Jane has displayed the determination and leadership necessary to be respected and valued by her team and the customer." – General Manager Support Services

Improvement oriented Corporate Services and Business Manager with a focus on profitability, service and effective human resource management. Able to garner support from staff and executive management, acting as a key coordination point to facilitate organisational and cultural change. Talent for recognising growth opportunities from a profit productivity and operational perspective.

VALUE OFFERED

1. Tender, Proposal and Contract Development
   Profit Maximisation
   Contract Negotiations
1. Executive Level Engagement

- Stakeholder, Account and Relationship Management
- Customer Relationship Management
- Operational, Service Delivery and Project Management

☐   ☐   ☐

BENCHMARKS AND MILESTONES

- Increased profit by 3% through development of strategic meeting plans, uniting a dispersed team through initiating training in dealing with difficult customers and demonstrating the necessity for effective communication with internal and external customers. Garnered support and broke down initial resistance through education and active listening. Training was rolled out across four departments and successful strategies subsequently adopted by finance and facilities department to reduce late invoicing and outstanding debtors payments by 55%.

- Instigated Strategic Planning Review to instil shared purpose into teams across four departments. Engaged with staff through a series of meetings to demonstrate necessity for united plans and purposes, information sharing and staff training. Resulted in dramatically reduced staff turnover rates from 30% to 5%, as well as adding five additional resources across the contract.

EMPLOYMENT NARRATIVE
Sample Workplace, Location
    03/2006–present
Executive Business Manager
Upon commencement, the challenges appeared daunting. Long standing customer difficulties combined with a four departmental team suffering lack of vision and failing to meet Key Performance Indicators prompted the need to develop a strategic plan and address customer shortfalls whilst improving profit, cash flow and staff morale and decreasing staff turnover.
Identified challenges including dissatisfied customers, backlogs in accounts payable and receivable, frequent staff turnover, and lack of shared vision.

- Instigated and rolled out a series of strategic planning review meetings with outcomes distributed to staff. Allowed staff to communicate frustrations and concerns whilst simultaneously facilitating training sessions in customer service, and dealing with difficult people. Staff turnover reduced dramatically from 30% to 5% with a marked upsurge in morale and a more cohesive unit.
- Increased profit by 3% whilst adding five additional resources across the contract through formulation and rollout of strategic planning, staff training, facilitating staff meetings and demonstrating how improvements could be made
- Received feedback from customer (reported to Senior Management) regarding their satisfaction with contract delivery within one year of my appointment, after reporting dissatisfaction in previous years

SNAPSHOT
Company: Sample employer is the largest provider of Defence services in Australia and provides Defence Support under the xxxx Contract

Budget: $7m pa, with additional $3-$7m Project Managed Works added throughout the financial year
Reported to: General Manager Land Business Unit)

- Recognised poor management of tenders for project work resulting in disgruntled client. Arranged two staff and myself to be trained in formal Defence procurement guidelines, implementing these into all project processes. Subsequently managed an additional $3 million in project work (estimated $7m in 2010/2011 financial year) managed throughout the entire tender process, enabling staff in following years to manage this process with minimal input from me

- Prepared and presented case to HR Manager with a view to securing increased retention bonuses for key staff as well as suggesting alternate strategies such as salary sacrifice to improve staff take home salary. Dramatic increases in staff morale and reduction in staff turnover of 25%
- Resolved challenging workplace bullying and aggressive communication behaviour which had impacted poorly upon team morale, through a series of meetings to inform colleagues their behaviour was unacceptable, maintaining professional and composed demeanour. Staff reported dramatic improvements in communications in and between teams and with the customer
- Empowered Head Gardener (Aboriginal Elder) during the recruitment and management of two grounds maintenance staff, as well as encouraging him to liaise with relevant stakeholders in relation to the performance of his staff, with the Head Gardener assuming the role of management and supervising staff effectively

Sample workplace, location   2004–2006
Operations Manager
Upon commencement, identified challenges such as limited understanding amongst staff of contract requirements, few financial controls in place, many staff holding more than 300 hours in accrued leave and lack of written processes,. A combination of poor management performance of previous incumbent, inadequate contract resourcing and scope creep had contributed to high staff turnover, failure to meet Key Performance Indicators and low staff morale. Within the first year of taking on this role, profit within one department had increased to $5k from a previous $60k loss, increasing to $40k in the next two years, amplified staff morale and dramatically reduced turnover and record levels of productivity.

- Garnered support from staff via a series of meetings utilising effective communication to ensure staff felt they had been heard, and used change management principles to change behaviour and plan for improvements resulting in improved morale and reduced turnover in Emergency services staff from 20% to nil over the next two years

- Improved morale and staff productivity through introduction of employee of the month awards, including staff nomination of colleagues for these awards

- Reduced accrued annual leave of emergency staff from a total of more than 1200 hours to almost zero through recommending and implementing flex time, as well as writing and submitting a successful contract change proposal to gain additional funding for emergency staff within the contract, enabling current staff to take leave as required

- Turned around operations department losses of $60,000 per annum to $5,000 profit within the first year, increasing annually by $40,000 and resulting in a $400K profit in 2009 through introducing processes to annually review pricing and marketing of services

Sample Workplace, location   08/2004−12/2004
Human Resources Consultant
Recognised challenges associated with previously implemented unlimited sick leave policy resulting in eighty staff on sick leave for over 6 months with detrimental cost to the company, low morale amongst teams
Within months this challenge had been overcome.
    Overcame Union opposition through meetings to generate understanding and invoke stakeholder buy-in
    As a result 83% of the staff that had been on long term sick leave returned to work within two months of policy implementation,
    Identified large numbers of staff whom had been on sick leave for over six months. Arranged meetings with Union representatives, Supervisors, Managers and employee representatives to discuss impacts of situation

* Formulated and wrote policy documents to summarise how unlimited sick leave should work, working with the Rehabilitation Coordinator, company GP and Supervisors to develop workable processes

Prior to 2004

Similar Workplace, 1/2003−01/2004
Human Resources Manager

Sample Workplace, 11/2001−01/2003
Manager Ernest Henry Mine Village

Sample Workplace 04/2001−11/2001
Facilities Manager

Sample Workplace, 07/2000−04/2001
Finance and Administration Manager

Sample Workplace, 10/1996−07/2000
Finance and Administration Manager

EDUCATION AND TRAINING

Master of Business Administration
Charles Sturt University

Graduate Certificate in Management
University of New England

Graduate Diploma in Conflict Resolution
Currently enrolled

REFERENCES
Available upon request

CHAPTER 17 - MORE ABOUT COVER LETTERS

These seem to be a source of concern for many job seekers, when really; the truth is that if your resume is well written, and achievement packed, the cover letter should be comparatively easy to write.

Use a standard cover letter layout (refer sample) below and then play to your strengths, otherwise known as achievements.

Even better is if you can weave keywords from the job ad into the letter, and address your cover letter specifically to their specifications.

Then of course there is the old favourite, demonstrating that you have done some research on the company and mentioning this within the letter:

This one worked quite well and with a bit of tweaking, Tim tells me he got job interviews one for one:

Mr. Tim Example
PO Box 0000
EXAMPLE SUBURB QLD 0000
Tele: +61 7 1234 5678
Mobile: +61 444 123 456

16 August 2013
Fictitious Limited
PO Box 0000
Wellesley Street
AUCKLAND   NEW ZEALAND
Email: sample@sample.com

Dear Sir/Madam

RE: MARKETING DIRECTOR REF NO: 44046SK

The educational background, experience, and skills listed in your recent advertisement on www.seek.com.au are only the beginning of what I can bring to this role.

I have a solid history of producing marketing and management results in an aquaculture environment and have developed, promoted and marketed several aquaculture projects. In my role with Phillips Foods Inc., I was responsible for the introduction of their core product, Pasteurised Crabmeat into the Australian market and for new value added product development from conception to commercial manufacture.

The key responsibilities in this role included the development and management of strategic relationships within the private sector and governmental organisations and development, implementation and review of strategy and research into market issues and emerging trends.

I deal effectively with clients, executives, and other stakeholders, and have supervised and managed foreign staff. I also have the ability to troubleshoot and provide solutions, all of these achievements are essential to companies that must compete in today's difficult economy.

My resume is enclosed as proof that I meet all the criteria listed in your advertisement and an interview would give me the chance to further demonstrate my unique strengths. I am available for an interview at a time of your convenience.

Sincerely,

<u>Mr. Tim X</u>

CHAPTER 18 – JOB INTERVIEW TIPS AND TRICKS

7 Easy Steps to Improve your Interviewing Skills

In the midst of technological advancement nowadays, the "back-to-basics" rule still applies when it comes to getting a job. It does not matter if you are planning to apply for a million-dollar company or a small, independent firm. When you face an interviewer, it all boils down to how you present yourself. This is the deciding factor on whether you will get hired or not.

So you have distributed your resume to prospective employers and you have determined the correct job to apply for. The next step is to schedule the job interview.

You can make the acquaintance of the assistant or the receptionist when you schedule for the interview, either by phone or personally. Be friendly and polite, as these people might provide information that can be essential to getting that job or, even just give you a background of the company or your prospective boss.

Finally, you show up for the interview.
The basic traits of being prompt, how you speak and carry yourself and even how you dress are all factors that contribute in making a lasting impression that will eventually get you hired.

Here are 7 easy steps on how you can improve your interviewing skills:

1.) Prepare for the interview.
First, dress appropriately. Once the interviewer walks into the room, or once you walk into the room to be interviewed, your appearance will be the first thing making an impact. Dress appropriately; check your grooming and your posture. Read the chapter on dressing for success!

Secondly, practice basic courtesy. Know where the interview will be held and be there with ample time to prepare yourself before the scheduled interview. Turn your phone off to avoid unnecessary distractions.

2.) Research.

Make full use of all resources to make sure that you know the basics about the company. You would not want to be caught unprepared when asked about how you heard or what you know about the company that you are applying for.

Learn about your potential employer. In your mind, develop a clear company profile.

Ensure that you prepared answers to a few basic questions, but do not sound scripted. This happens when you rehearse what you will be saying word for word. It is enough that you have an overview of what you will impart to the interviewer, and it is better to be spontaneous.

3.) Be cool.

Step forward so that you are now seated and the interview is about to begin. Make a great first impression by maintaining eye contact, giving the interviewer a firm handshake, a friendly smile and a polite greeting. Sit only when you are asked to do so and do not forget to thank the interviewer for taking time off of his or her busy schedule to interview you.
Make sure to start on a positive note and set the proper expectations.

4.) Do not sell yourself short.

In the course of the interview, answer the questions briefly and accurately. The key is to be honest.
Make sure that as a prospective employee, you impart to your future employer what you really are and how you can add value to the company, not the other way around. Stay positive and do not give a bad impression about your previous employer.

If you are applying for your first job, do not let your lack of experience hinder you from gaining the advantage against more experienced applicants. What you lack in experience, make up for in confidence and eagerness to learn.

You may also put yourself in the employer's shoes. Ask yourself, if I were on the other side of this desk, what qualities should I look for in a potential employee? Would I profit if he works for me and can he contribute to the development of the company?

Do not be afraid to sell yourself but do not be overconfident. Just project an air that you are sure of yourself and your capabilities.

5.) Ask questions.

Should you encounter a difficult interviewer, do not be intimidated. One who does not let you put in a word edgewise should be lightly reminded that you should do most of the talking since he is the one who needs to learn more about you.

6.) Wrap it up.
As you near the end of the interview, make sure that all bases are covered. Now is not the time to discuss or even ask about the salary and the benefits that you will receive once employed? There is ample time for that once you do get the position and you are discussing the job offer.

Wrap things up by summarising your strengths and pointing out your positive traits. Finally, as you end the interview, be sure to thank the interviewer again for his or her time, thus leaving a lasting impression.

7.) Follow up.

Send that all-important thank you note after the interview. Thank the interviewer for the time that he took with you and for giving you that opportunity. Make sure that you know who to contact for follow-up of the results.

A lot of research has been made about the interviewing process.

Here is a brief run-through:

First, you make a schedule for the interview.

Then, you are there in the office and you are seen by the interviewee.
The interview itself then transpires.

Next is the closing, then you follow-up with a thank-you-note. You eventually get accepted and you discuss, negotiate for and sign-up the job offer.

You may notice that the interviewing takes up a great deal of the getting-hired process, so you might as well polish up your interviewing skills on your way to getting that dream job.

How to Follow Up on All Contacts

If you are still in the job search process, it is extremely important to follow up on all contacts. It is not good to just sit and wait for results to come pouring in when you think that you've already done your part because your contact information has been distributed. Consider two men applying for a prime position at a company. After the interview, the first applicant just sits around waiting to hear from his prospective employer.

On the other hand, the second applicant distributes his contact information to some people that he met in the company. Furthermore, applicant number two does a follow-up on the results of the job interview a few days later. The first applicant has not been heard from, because he just relies on the basic "We'll call you" routine. Who do you think will have a greater chance of getting the job?

Even though the first applicant is more qualified, since he did not follow up or even send a thank you note to the interviewer, in the end, he does not get the job.

If you are still waiting for that job offer and you do not follow up on your contacts, your chances of getting hired become slimmer. In business, following up on all of your contacts is a sure-fire way to spread the word about you, your business sense and expanding your horizons.

If you are still looking for a job, here are some tips on how to follow up on your contacts:

* Send a thank you note right after the interview, ideally after a couple of days. This is a way of getting the prospective employer to hear from you again. Should you not get hired for the current position that they offer, someone from that company will likely keep your information on file for future consideration.

* Make sure that you leave your mobile and landline number, e-mail address and home address so that prospective employers will have no excuse for not getting in touch with you.

* Be accurate in getting the contact information of perspective employers. In return, when you place their information on any letter that you send out (i.e. resumes, thank you notes) avoid typographical errors and make sure that you have their names correct, to see to it that everything is in order.

* Some companies do take a look at your character references so alert the people on your list that they might receive a call from your prospective employers.

* Always be positive. Should you not get hired for a particular position, you may ask the people from that company for referrals to other companies or at least keep you in mind for future hiring. If you are currently in business, whether you are just starting out or in the midst of expanding, you also need to make sure to follow up on all important contacts. For example, you go to a corporate event and you have distributed a lot of business cards. Do not stop there. These people might eventually bring big business to your company so it is important to build up a strong business

relationship with them.

Here are some tips on following up on your contacts if you are already in business:

* Send thank you notes to current and future customers. This rule does not just apply to people applying for a job. This is much more helpful for those who are already in business, as a simple thank you note would remind customers of which company they are dealing with and your brand name will be imprinted on their minds. This practice should send more business your way.

* Send follow up messages. If you are in sales, it is good to follow up on existing buyers who are most likely to purchase your products again.

You might also want to personalise any correspondence that you send out as this leaves the customers feeling as if they know you personally. This should lead you to earning their trust, which in turn leaves the customer feeling secure that you are handling efficiently whatever business it is that they throw your way.

* Make sure that you follow up swiftly and promptly. The rule of thumb is to reply fast, fast, fast. Whether it is a solution to a problem or sending out an order or replying to a letter, responding quickly to a customer is the easiest way for them to think of you and your company in a positive way.

How to Create a List of Warm Contacts
Usually when you are looking for a job, you would ask for help from family and friends. You would contact these people to ask for information on current job openings, business opportunities and tips.
Your family, relatives and friends belong to your warm contact list. The warm contact list is the list of people with whom you have or

had some personal association. A former classmate, officemate or neighbour may belong to your warm contact list.
Who may be included in your warm contact list? Here are a number of selections.

* Relatives and Friends
These people are always willing to help you in your job search or business venture. They will be able to provide you information if they have some, or refer you to trustworthy people who will be able to help you. If they will introduce you to some of their contacts, they can surely provide honest information to you regarding the person you are going to associate with.

* Members of the church, political party, social club or university group

You probably did not expect it, but people who share the same faith, beliefs or hobbies may also help you with finding a job. You may have a different career from theirs, but they might know somebody who is in the same field or will be able to help you in your career.
However, depending on your level of association with them, they may think twice about giving their opinion or thoughts about their contacts. Their opinion can sometimes help you in making a strategy on how to approach and ask for help from their contacts.

* People who sell you things
You may think that your relationship with these people is purely based on trading goods and services, then paying for them. However, people who sell you things are also sources of information when networking.

Since these people sell their goods to different types of persons, they may have associated with somebody who belongs to the same field as you do, or have heard information about your target job from their other clients.

These people will also be happy to help you, since they know that maintaining a pleasant relationship with you means a stable business. Also, if you have a good job means you have increased your purchasing power, and then it could also mean that you may purchase more from them.

* Former employers, colleagues or co-workers
Maintaining a good relationship with previous employers and colleagues has more benefits than you can imagine. This is the reason that most people try their best to iron out any difficulties with their previous employers even if they are no longer associated with the company. Aside from the possibility that your potential employer will call previous employers when they review your job history, former employers and colleagues are also a good source of information related to that field.

When you ask for help from family and friends, there is the possibility that the information that they can give to you is just from another source. They may not be able to give you first-hand information or detailed information unless they also work in the same field that you came from or would like to go into.

This is very different when you consult former employers and colleagues from the same sector. They will be able to provide you with valuable information and may be able to clarify such information and answer your questions.

* Members of your professional organisation
If you belong to a professional organisation related to the field in which you are looking for a job, you can consult the organisation for current posting from the members. If you don't belong to any, consider joining one since this will be beneficial to you career growth.
A professional organisation can provide you unbiased information on current job openings from its members. The organization can also give you details on the company profile and even on current market and career trends.

These are the most important people that you should include when creating a list of your warm contacts. It is better if you contact them all so you can have as many options in your job search. When you talk to them, tell them that you are actively seeking a job.

Jobseeker FAQs on Thank you notes

Career advisers tell jobseekers to send a thank you note after an interview. To address the most frequently asked questions on how and what to send in a thank you note, here are some giveaways. Won't the employer think that an applicant is desperate and a sissy applicant if he sends a thank-you letter?

Of course not. Rarely is an employer displeased to receive a thank-you letter. It is considered as a common way of showing politeness, a gesture of courtesy, one way to outshine the rest of the interviewees, and a way to keep your name upfront.

Will it not jeopardize the possibility of getting the job?
Not in most cases, but it could in some point of time. So why take the chance? The answer: Most employers waiver between the last two most promising applicants, a student and experienced officer for example, after the final interview for a certain position. But when the boss gets a thank-you letter from the student, it made all the difference. Because of that simple well-mannered gesture, the student lands the job.

Can it be handwritten or should it be typewritten?
I usually recommend a typewritten letter. However what is important is the thought of doing it, and the way it is written. It must be tailored to your prospective company and the officer who made the interview. Thus, respect is further established. However, if the company, interviewer or the position being applied calls for a formal business letter, then do so.

Will it be okay to e-mail the thank you note?
This depends on the company's culture. If the people in the company use e-mail in all of their communication and correspondence, then it should be acceptable. This will also apply

if the company is into fast decision making when hiring applicants.

Always remember that even if E-mails fit in with the culture of the company; it's still a better idea to follow up the email with a hard copy of your thank you.

So you can just save yourself from trouble since "anything goes" right?

NO. On the other side of the previous story, there are prospective applicants who were almost on the verge of being hired but suddenly hit the skids after sending in a sloppy, ill-fixed thank you letter, with many typographical errors and misspelled words. A large part of having good communication skills is being able to write effectively and companies do not need employees who have to be taught simple writing skills.

Will a borrowed thank-you letter do?
Yes, borrowing is one thing. But make sure to look at the basic structure of the letter. Never plagiarise the entire letter as it may be applicable to the one person but not for the other. Surely, there are employers who can distinguish a thank-you note that has been copied or not.

If it was a panel interview should thank you letters be sent to all interviewers?
Frankly, that's the best. The same letter to each is as essential as making one for each. All you have to do is edit some phrases for individuality in case the interviewers bump in to each other and compare the notes they received.

How soon should a thank-you note be sent?
The golden rule is to send thank you notes within 24 hours after the interview.

Will it still be okay to mail the thank you note if the hiring decision will be made sooner than when the mailed thank you note is received?

Come to think of it, if the mail is too pre-historic for the hiring decision makers, then find a much more speedy way: it can be via e-mail, fax, express delivery or personal delivery. In fact, if you have hand delivered the thank you note, it can leave a great impression.

What if there's already an offer before even sending the thank you notes?

It's still better to send the thank you notes as this can be used to accept or decline the offer. This could also be a confirmation of your agreement and/or understanding of the offer they have given (salary, benefits, other compensation, starting date, annual leave, etc.), this way any discrepancies can be straightened out before even starting for the job.

Always find a way to make it as personalised as possible. Try to think laterally or outside the square, you may even adapt what you have observed the interviewer has in the office during the interview. Sending an article that you think the interviewer could be interested in is also another suggestion.

Whatever method you use, make it fast and professional.

CHAPTER 19 – BONUS SECTION

POWER WORDS THAT SELL
ACTION VERBS BY CATEGORY
*** Please note: Changed to Australian Spelling ***

Creative
acted customised illustrated painted
adapted designed imagined perceived
applied developed innovated performed
began devised initiated photographed
built directed instituted planned
chartered displayed integrated revised
combined drew introduced revitalised
composed entertained invented shaped
conceived established memorised sketched
conceptualised fashioned modelled solved
condensed formulated modified transformed
created generated originated

Fiscal/Data
adjusted calculated earned prepared
allocated checked eliminated programmed
analysed computed enumerated projected
anticipated conserved equated realised
appraised corrected estimated reconciled
assessed decreased forecasted reduced
audited determined managed researched
balanced developed marketed retrieved
budgeted disbursed measured simplified
calculated documented planned slashed

Helping
acted collaborated facilitated referred
adapted contributed familiarised rehabilitated

advocated cooperated furthered represented
aided counselled guided resolved
answered demonstrated helped simplified
arranged diagnosed inspired supplied
assisted educated insured supported
cared for encouraged intervened volunteered
circumvented enhanced motivated
clarified ensured prevented
coached expedited provided

Interpersonal

argued (lawyers) corresponded interpreted recommended
adapted counselled interviewed reconciled
addressed debated involved recorded
advertised defined joined recruited
advised described judged referred
arbitrated developed lectured reinforced
arranged directed listened rendered
articulated discussed marketed reported
authored drafted mediated resolved
clarified edited moderated responded
collaborated elicited negotiated solicited
communicated enlisted observed specified
composed explained outlined spoke
condensed expressed participated suggested
conducted formulated persuaded summarised
conferred furnished presented synthesised
consulted incorporated promoted translated
contacted influenced proposed wrote
conveyed interacted publicised
convinced interfaced reasoned

Investigative

accumulated conserved evaluated interviewed
adhered correlated examined invented
analysed critiqued explored investigated
ascertained described extracted located
assimilated detected extrapolated measured
clarified determined formulated monitored
classified diagnosed gathered navigated

collected discovered identified organised
compared documented inspected
compiled enumerated interpreted

Management/Leadership

accelerated contemporised generated oversaw
accommodated contracted handled planned
achieved controlled headed presided
administered converted hired prioritised
alleviated coordinated hosted produced
analysed decided improved recommended
appointed delegated incorporated rejuvenated
approved developed increased reorganised
assigned directed initiated replaced
asserted dispatched inspected restored
attained eliminated instituted reviewed
augmented emphasised led scheduled
authorised enacted managed secured
built enforced merged selected
chaired enhanced motivated streamlined
considered established organised strengthened
consolidated evaluated originated supervised
contemporised executed overhauled terminated

Mentoring

adapted critiqued fostered motivated
advised demonstrated guided persuaded
briefed developed individualised set goals
clarified enabled influenced simulated
coached encouraged informed taught
communicated evaluated instilled tested
conducted explained instructed trained
consulted facilitated lectured transmitted
coordinated focused motivated tutored

Organisational

accumulated distributed operated reviewed
adopted executed ordered routed
approved experimented organised scheduled
arranged filed prepared screened
catalogued generated processed set up
categorised grouped procured standardised
charted implemented provided submitted
classified incorporated purchased supplied
coded inspected recorded systematised
collated logged registered updated
collected maintained reserved validated
compiled monitored responded verified
corrected obtained retained

☐

CHAPTER 20 - CONCLUSION

When you are looking for a job, having the right tools at your disposal is extremely important. Those tools include having a killer resume along with a compelling cover letter that will help prospective employers choose you over anyone else.

I have given you a lot of advice about how to craft your resume to put your best foot forward to make you look great for the job and compel them to call you first over any other applicant. What you need to do is stand out over the competition and be sure that you are the one that gets the interview!

There is a lot that goes into making a resume that works. When you have all of the components in place, you can make a resume that works for you and one that will help you get a job. And, after all, that is your end result, now isn't it?

Take your time in writing your resume and be sure that it reflects who you are and what you can do. Let your resume speak for you and your abilities and be sure to follow up on all of the places you have submitted your resume to.

Whether you borrowed this eBook, purchased it or were lucky enough to access it for free during my free promotion period – why not join my book buyers list?

I'll send you tips and info about once a month, and you'll be the first to know when my next two books are released. In coming months I'll be releasing two titles including: "Job Interviews Made Easy" and "Government Job Applications Made Easy" – Here's the link!

http://forms.aweber.com/form/03/890930203.htm

I hope you have found some benefit from the techniques detailed in this e-book. I love to hear from my readers, and welcome your questions and feedback – andrea@career-chick.com.au

But most of all – enjoy the journey and flourish and prosper! That is my wish for you – health, happiness, success and prosperity. To your job searching success.......

Andrea Drew
Author
www.career-chick.com.au (including blog)
www.an-exec-resume.com
www.andrea-drew.com
www.career-coach.net.au

ABOUT THE AUTHOR

Andrea Drew formed Impressive Resumes in 1998 and the business grew steadily over 13 years before Andrea sold the business to new management in 2011. She has a lifetime love of writing which she uses in the preparation and writing of resumes, copywriting and other entrepreneurial endeavours. With a background in Human Resources and Recruitment, Andrea has worked in helping people with jobs since 1993. Her roles included: culling CV's, arranging interviews, assessing resumes; writing marketing material; writing tenders; editing, proofreading and rewriting large documents.

Andrea is currently studying prior to gaining accreditation as a Certified Advanced Resume Writer and is a member of Career Directors International and the Association of Online Resume and Career Professionals.

You can follow Andrea on Twitter here:
http://twitter.com/ImpressiveCV
Or via her various websites here:
www.career-chick.com.au
www.an-exec-resume.com
www.andrea-drew.com

Andrea Drew

www.ingramcontent.com/pod-product-compliance
Lightning Source LLC
Chambersburg PA
CBHW051219170526
45166CB00005B/1970